The Lord's Table

A Help to the Right Observance of the Holy Supper

by Rev. Andrew Murray

DESTINY IMAGE® PUBLISHERS, INC.
P.O. Box 310, Shippensburg, PA 17257-0310

"Speaking to the Purposes of God for this Generation and for the Generations to Come."

This book and all other Destiny Image, Revival Press, Mercy Place, Fresh Bread, Destiny Image Fiction, and Treasure House books are available at Christian bookstores and distributors worldwide.

For a U.S. bookstore nearest you, call 1-800-722-6774.

For more information on foreign distributors, call 717-532-3040.

Or reach us on the Internet: www.destinyimage.com

ISBN 10: 0-7684-2473-9
ISBN 13: 978-0-7684-2473-7

For Worldwide Distribution, Printed in the U.S.A.

1 2 3 4 5 6 7 8 9 10 11 / 09 08 07

Contents

Part I

The Week before the Supper

Part II

The Communion Sabbath

Part III

The Week after the Supper

PREFACE

On the use of this little volume I would fain say two things which lie upon my heart.

The first is this: that the Christian who desires to make use of it must not be content merely to read and to understand the portion for the day, but must take time to meditate upon it and to appropriate it. I am convinced that one chief cause why some do not grow more in grace is that they do not take time to hold converse with the Lord in secret. Spiritual, divine truth does not thus become our possession at once. Although I understand what I read, although I consent heartily to it, although I receive it, it may speedily fade away and be forgotten, unless by private meditation I give it time to become fixed and rooted in me, to become united and identified with me. Christians, give yourselves, give your Lord time to transfer His heavenly thoughts to your inner, spiritual life. When you have read a portion, set yourselves in silence before God. Take time to remain before Him until He has made His word living and powerful in your souls. Then does it become the life and the power of your life.

And this brings me to the second remark which I desire to make. It is this: that the Christian must take special care that he do not suffer himself to be led away from the Word of God by the many manuals which in our days are seeing the light. These books will have this result, — whenever a man seeks his instruction only in what the writer has to say, he then becomes accustomed to take everything at second hand. These books can become a blessing to the reader only when they bring him always to that portion of God's Word which is treated of in order that he may meditate further upon it himself as from the mouth of God. Christians, there is in the Word of God an incredible power. The blessing which lies hid in it is inconceivable. See to it that when you have read a portion you always return to that passage of the Scriptures of which an explanation is given. Receive that not as the word of man, but, as it is in truth, the Word of God, which works mightily in those that believe. Hold fellowship with God through the Word. Take time to speak with Him about it, to give an answer to Him concerning it. Then shall you understand what the Lord Jesus says: "The words which I speak unto you, they are spirit and life." Then shall Word and sacrament gloriously work together, to make you increase in prayer and in the life of God.

That the Eternal God may bless this little volume also, to make His children learn His own Word, is the prayer of the author for all his readers.

A. M.

Part 1

The Week Before the Supper

The Lord's Table

My God, and is Thy table spread?
And does Thy cup with love o'erflow?
Thither be all Thy children led,
And let them all its sweetness know.

Hail, sacred feast, which Jesus makes!
Rich banquet of His flesh and blood!
Thrice happy he who here partakes
That sacred stream, that heavenly food!

O let Thy table honored be,
And furnished well with joyful guests;
And may each soul salvation see
That here its sacred pledges tastes.

Let crowds approach with hearts prepared,
With hearts inflamed let all attend;
Nor, when we leave our Father's board,
The pleasure or the profit end.

Revive Thy drooping Churches, Lord!
And bid our drooping graces live;
And more, that energy afford,
A Saviour's love alone can give.

—Philip Doddridge

Sabbath Morning

The Divine Invitation

"Behold, I have made ready my dinner. All things are ready. Come to the marriage."—Matthew 22:4.

Let the King of Heaven and Earth say this to you. In honor of His Son He has prepared a great supper. There the Son bears His human nature. There are all the children of men, dear and precious to the Father, and He has caused them to be invited to the great festival of the Divine love. He is prepared to receive and honor them there as guests and friends. He will feed them with

His heavenly food. He will bestow upon them the gifts and energies of everlasting life.

O my soul, thou also hast received this heavenly invitation. To be asked to eat with the King of Glory: how it behooves thee to embrace and be occupied with this honor. How desirous must you be to prepare yourself for this feast. How you must long that you should be in dress and demeanor, and language and disposition, all that may be rightly expected of one who is invited to the court of the King of kings.

Glorious invitation! I think of the *banquet* itself and what it has cost the great God to prepare it. To find food for angels: for this only one word was necessary. But to prepare for man upon this accursed earth a banquet of heavenly food—that cost Him much. Nothing less than the life and blood of His Son, to take away the curse and to open up to them the right and the access to heavenly blessings. Nothing less than the body and the blood of the Son of God could give life to lost men. O my soul, ponder the wonders of this royal banquet.

I think of the *invitation*. It is as free, as wide as it could be, "without money and without price." The poorest and the most unworthy are called to it. And so urgent and cordial is it. Not less cordial is the love which invites to it, the love which longs after sinners and takes delight in entertaining and blessing them.

I think of the *blessing* of the banquet. The dying are fed with the power of a heavenly life, the lost are restored to their places in the Father's house, those that thirst after God are satisfied with God Himself and with His love.

Glorious invitation! With adoration I receive it, and prepare myself to make use of it. I have read of those who hold themselves excused because they are hindered, — one by his merchandise, another by his work, and a third by his domestic happiness. I have heard the voice which has said, "I say unto you, that none of these men which were bidden shall taste of My supper." Under the conviction that He who so cordially invites me is the Holy One, who will not suffer Himself to be mocked, I will prepare myself to lay aside all thoughtlessness, to withdraw myself from the seductions of the world; and with all earnestness to yield obedience to the voice of the heavenly love. I will remain in quiet meditation and in fellowship with the children of God, to keep myself free from all needless anxiety about the world, and as an invited guest, to meet my God with real hunger and quiet joy. He Himself will not withhold from me His help in this work.

PRAYER

Eternal God, I have received the good tidings that there is room also for me at the table of Thy Son. With grateful thanks I receive thy invitation, God of all grace. I hunger for Thy bread, O Lord. My soul thirsts for God. For the living God my flesh and my heart cry out. When shall I enter and appear before the face of God?

Lord, graciously bestow upon me this week a real blessing in the way of preparation. Let the sight of my sinfulness humble me deeply and take away from me all hope in myself. Let the sight of Thy grace again encourage me and fill me with confidence and gladness. Do Thou Thyself stir up within me a mighty desire for the Bridegroom, for the precious Jesus, without whom there could be no feast. And may it be manifest in me this week that I am full of the thought that I have an invitation to eat bread in the house of my God with his only-begotten and well-beloved Son. Lord, grant this for Jesus' sake.

Lord Jesus, thou hast taught me: "God is a spirit, and they that worship Him must worship Him in spirit and in truth." Lord, spiritual worship we cannot bring: but Thou wilt bestow upon us Thy Spirit. I entreat thee, Lord, to grant the working of the Spirit. The blessing of the Supper is a high spiritual blessing. The invisible God will there come very near to us and will very mightily impart the gift of eternal life to those who have the spiritual capacity for it. Only the spiritual mind can enjoy the spiritual blessing. Thou knowest how deeply I fail in this receptiveness for a full blessing. But grant, I pray thee, that the Holy Spirit may this week dwell and work in me with special power. I will surrender myself for this end to Him and to His guidance, in order that He may overcome in me the spirit of the world and renew my inner life to inherit from my God a new blessing. Lord, let Thy Spirit work mightily within me.

And as I thus pray for myself I pray also for the whole congregation. Grant, Lord, in behalf of all thy children an overflowing outpouring of Thy Spirit, in order that this Supper may really be for all of us a time of quickening and renewal of our energies. Amen.

My Prayer for Today:

Monday Morning

Monday Morning
The Preparation

"Where wilt Thou that we go and make ready, that thou mayest eat the passover?" "He will himself show you a large upper room furnished and ready, and there make ready for us." "If thou set thine heart aright, then stretch out thine hands toward Him."—Mark 4:12, 15; Job 11:13.

The greater a work is that a man undertakes the more important is the preparation. Four days before the Passover the Israelite had to make his preparations. The Lord Jesus also desired that care should be taken to obtain an upper room furnished and ready where the Passover might be prepared. When I am called upon to meet my God and to sit down at His table, I will see to it that I do not approach it unprepared. Otherwise I should dishonor Him and lose the blessing which is destined for me, and cover my soul with heavy guilt.

For a right preparation two things are necessary. The first is this: that my heart should be occupied and filled with Him who has invited me, and with all the glorious blessing which He is to bestow upon me. Great thoughts of Jesus and large expectations of what His love will do will set the heart aglow and be the best preparation for meeting Himself.

The second part of preparation is to consider if I shall be a worthy guest, acceptable and welcome to the Lord of the Feast: that is if I am really an invited guest willing and prepared to come to the table according to the law of the King in such a manner as He will approve of. To cherish mean thoughts of myself, and no more expectation from myself or of any good in me, and out of this to have deep-rooted renunciation of myself in order to be willing to live through Jesus alone—this is the attitude of soul which leads to a blessed observance of the Supper.

Man obtains nothing without laying out time upon it. Even where free grace is to do everything apart from our working, we must give it time to carry out its work in our hearts. It is only when in secrecy I resolve with myself to look to Jesus until my desires become truly operative within me, that I shall be really prepared for the banquet. It is only when I deal trustfully with Him in the ordinary converse of the hidden and the daily life, that I can expect extraordinary blessing from public communion with Him at His table. Yea, hunger and thirst cannot be awakened simply when I see the table. It is in the conflict of the preceding life that hunger and thirst are aroused. Only for such is the table a feast. May this quickening not be wanting to me in this preparation.

But, alas! just as little as it was my work to prepare the table with its food, am I in a position to prepare myself as a guest for the feast. The Lord who says, "All things are ready," has also prepared the wedding garment. He Himself will clothe the guests and prepare them for His feast. Therefore I will ask Him for this also. It was of the Lord that the disciples asked: "Where wilt thou that we prepare the passover?" Of Him also I may and will ask: "Lord,how wilt thou that I prepare the passover?" This week I will continue in quiet meditations and prayer at His feet, with eye and heart fixed upon Him. I know assuredly that I shall find what is needful for me in celebrating this feast.

PRAYER

Lord, deliver me from all superficiality and light-mindedness in drawing near to Thy table. Too often have I supposed that it is self-evident I must use again the Lord's Supper. I have considered too little how needful it was to take the stones out of the way, when the Lord Himself shall come to prepare His way and make His path straight. I fancied that it was a light thing to receive blessing. Lord, forgive me this error. Do Thou Thyself enable my soul to understand what is meant by saying that sinful man shall meet his God. Do Thou Thyself work within me true conscientiousness and eagerness to lay bare and to lay aside every sin, and trust myself wholly to Thee with a real surrender of the whole soul and of all its powers.

Lord Jesus, hear, I beseech Thee, this my petition. O Lord, grant that I may not lose the blessing by thoughtlessness or idleness. O my Lord, how much has it cost Thee to prepare the table for me, and now even this is not enough. I must still ask Thee to prepare me for the table. I thank Thee for the joyful assurance which I have that Thou wilt do this. Therefore I place myself for this week in Thy hands, in order that by Thy working in me a right condition of soul may be brought into existence.

Monday Morning- The Preparation

Precious Lord, grant me the broken and contrite heart. And grant unto me to look up unto Thee with a living, active faith as my Friend, my Saviour, my All. Grant, Lord Jesus, that I also may be able to say: I have but one thought, one desire, and that is Jesus. So shall I be prepared with honor to the Father to glorify Thee by my cheerful confession that I desire nothing but Thee, and Thy wonderful love.

My Saviour, I depend upon Thee throughout this week. Work thou in me a true preparation for the Supper. I expect it from Thee. Amen.

My Prayer for Today:

My Prayer for Today:

Tuesday Morning

Tuesday Morning
The Host

"And He said unto them, With desire have I desired to eat this passover with you." "Behold, I stand at the door and knock: if any man bear My voice, and open the door, I will come in to him, and will sup with him, and he with Me."—Luke 22:15; Revelation 3:20.

The best preparation is—to look into the heart of Jesus. When you understand what He that sits on the throne desires for you, how He longs after you, what He has prepared for you, this will more than aught else set your desires and longings in motion, and impart to you the right preparation.

That Word of Jesus at the Paschal Table enables me to look into His heart. He knew that He must go from that feast to the Cross. He knew that His body must be broken, and His blood shed, in order that He might be really your Passover. He knew how in that night they should grieve and betray Him, and yet He says: "With desire have I desired to eat this passover with you." What a love this is! And Jesus is still the same. Even with you, poor sinner, He earnestly desires to eat the Passover. Yea, on the throne of Heaven, He looks forward with longing to the day of the Supper, to eat with you, and to quicken you. O man, let your sluggishness put you to shame: Jesus earnestly desires—Jesus greatly longs—to observe the Supper with you: He would not enjoy the food of heavenly life alone: He would fain eat of it along with you.

Or, we may think of it as that other word says: In order to observe the Supper with the soul, He stands at the door and knocks. Wonderful condescension! What is there in the vile sinner that the King of Heaven longs to sit down beside him? In order to hold a feast in my heart, Jesus stands at the door and knocks. Is not this inconceivable love? Is it not unspeakable blessing?

He would fain come in Himself. His presence is the special joy of the feast. And He Himself will hand to me and make me partaker of the heavenly food He brings to me. Even as the little weak infant, that does not know how to eat, is fed by its mother's hand, so will Jesus break for me the bread of Heaven, and impart to me what I have need of.

Glorious Paschal feast thus observed with Jesus: glorious Supper held with Jesus. He is the Entertainer: He is the Wedding Garment: He is also the Food. He knows precisely what I need: He knows what it is that has hindered me hitherto, and the love of Jesus has seen meet to impart to me at His table just that one thing which can satisfy my hunger. Dost Thou, Lord Jesus, earnestly desire to keep the Passover with me? I venture to answer: I also earnestly desire to observe the Supper with Thee. My whole heart longs for the Supper with Jesus.

There is nothing on earth that awakens love and rouses it to activity so powerfully as the thought of being desired and loved. Let me endeavor to conceive how true it is that I am an object of desire to the Son of God. He looks out to see whether I am coming to Him or not. With the deepest interest, He would know whether I come hungering after Him, so that He may be able to bestow much of His blessing upon me. That would be such a joy to His love. "Open thy mouth wide; I will fill it abundantly." Thus does He stir me up to earnest longings. His desire is toward me. My soul, believe and ponder this wonderful thought, until you feel drawn with overmastering force to give yourself over to Jesus, for the satisfaction of His desire toward you: then shall you too be satisfied.

PRAYER

Eternal Love, what am I that Thou shouldest desire to eat with me? Lord, it is too great a boon that Thou shouldest earnestly desire to eat with me: with me, who have desired so little to eat with Thee, who have longed so much more for the food that perisheth and for the fellowship of the world than for Thee and Thy heavenly bread. My Lord, give me so to feel the desire of Thy soul to eat with me, that my sluggishness and my unbelief shall be ashamed, and all that is within me may prepare to set my heart open with joy before Thee.

Yea, Lord, too long have I suffered Thee to stand at the door and knock: now will I open it to Thee. Make even my heart a banquet hall furnished and prepared where Thou mayest make ready the passover. Let the sight of Thy blood poured out for me be to me the full assurance of redemption. Let the eating of the Lamb fill me with the power of a heavenly life. Let the eating with Thee be fellowship with Thyself and Thy love be the joy of my soul. Blessed Jesus, let the love of Thy heart which draws Thee to me, also draw me to Thee.

My Saviour, it is this especially that I crave at Thy hand: unveil to me the love of Thy heart that makes Thee long so much after me. I know that this is one of the secret things that remain for Thy dearest friends, and I hardly dare reckon myself amongst them. And yet, Lord, may I venture to do so? Grant me, I pray Thee, one more glance into Thy heart, that I may know how earnestly Thou dost desire to eat with me. Let my soul conceive what it is to have me at Thy table with this great desire. Thou wouldst have me as Thine own possession. Thou wouldst enter into the deepest communion with me. Thou wouldst communicate Thyself to me. Thou wouldst become one with me. Thou wouldst have me for Thyself. My Jesus, if this be really so, cause me to feel it. Let not my heart remain in darkness. Then shall I turn away from all else, and my life shall be filled with one supreme desire—to eat with Jesus, my King and my Friend. Precious Jesus, grant that it may indeed be so. Amen.

My Prayer for Today:

My Prayer for Today:

Wednesday Morning

Wednesday Morning
Self-Examination

"But let a man prove himself, and so let him eat of the bread and drink of the cup." "Try your own selves, whether ye be in the faith: prove your own selves. Or know ye not as to your own selves, that Jesus Christ is in you? unless indeed, ye be reprobate."—1 Corinthians 11:28; 2 Corinthians 13:5.

No one may eat of the bread without self-examination. The danger of "unworthy communicating" is indeed very great. The sin of "making oneself guilty of the body and blood of the Lord" is very grave. The possibility of eating judgment unto oneself is very fearful (read I Corinthians 11:27-30). Everyone who is truly desirous of a blessing at the table will be very willing to yield obedience to the command of our Lord; "Try your own selves:" "Prove your own selves."

The problem of self-examination is simple. According to the apostle, there are but two conditions, either Jesus Christ is in you, or ye are reprobate: one of two. There is no third condition. The life of Christ in you may still be weak; but if you are truly born again and a child of God, Christ is in you. And then as a child you have access to the table of the Father and a share in the children's bread.

But if Christ is not in you, you are "reprobate." Nothing that is in you, nothing that you do, or are, or even desire and wish to be, makes you acceptable to God. The God against whom you have sinned inquires only about one thing: whether you have received His Son. "He that hath the Son hath the life." With nothing less than this can He be content: with this He is fully satisfied. If Christ is in you, you are acceptable to the Father. But if Christ is not in you, you are at the very same moment "reprobate." You have come in to the Lord's Supper without the wedding garment: your lot must be in the outermost darkness. You are unworthy. You eat judgment to yourself. You make yourself "guilty of the body and blood of the Lord."

Wednesday Morning - Self Examination

Reader, how is it with you? What will God say of you when He sees you at the table? Will God look upon you as one of His children, who are very heartily welcome to Him at His table, or as an intruder who has no right to be at His table? You would not for a moment sit down at the table of a man on earth if you were aware that you were not welcome to him, or if you thought that he did not willingly see you there. Surely, then, you would not dream of sitting down at the table of God, while it is still possible that He may look upon you with anger, as one who is desecrating His ordinance. Reader, pray answer this question: What will God say of you when He beholds you at His table? You are one of two things: you are either a true believer and a child of God, or you are not. If you are a child of God, you have a right to the table and eat the bread of the Father, however feeble you may be. But if you are not a child of God, no true believer, you have no right to it. You may not go forward to it.

Reader, try your own self, whether you are in the faith: prove yourself. And should it appear that you do not yet have Christ, then even to-day receive Him. There is still time. Without delay give yourself to Christ: in Him you have a right to the Lord's Table.

Prayer

Search me, O God, and know my heart, try me and know my thoughts, and see if there be any wicked way in me and lead me in the way that is everlasting. Lord, Thou knowest how deceitful the heart is, far above all things. But, Lord, Thou knowest the heart, even my heart. And now I come to Thee, Omniscient One, and set my heart before Thee with the prayer: Lord, make me know whether Jesus Christ is in me, or whether I am still without Him, and reprobate before Thee.

Of old, Thou Thyself didst see to it that hypocrites should be cast out from the midst of Thy people. Thou didst point out Achan. Thou didst make known the man who dipped his hand in the dish with Thy Son. Thou didst detect Ananias. Thou art the King who comest in to scrutinize the guests that have sat down, and who sayest: "Friend, how camest thou in hither, not being in the wedding garment?" Thou art still mighty to search the hearts. Lord, hear now the supplication of Thy people, and purge Thy congregation. Let the life of the Spirit become so powerful that all doubts shall vanish, and Thy children know and confess that Christ is in them. Let Thy presence in their midst effect such a joy and such a reverence that mere confessors with the lips shall be afraid, and the self-righteous be brought to detection. Lord, make it known to many who are still content in uncertainty, whether Christ is in them or whether they are reprobate.

Great God, make this known to me. Is Jesus Christ in me? Let the Holy Spirit give me the blessed assurance of this. Then shall I sit down with confidence as Thy child at Thy table.

And if Jesus Christ is still not in me, and I am still without Christ and reprobate before Thee, Thou merciful One, make this known to me. Make me willing to know this, and not to draw near to Thy table except that Jesus Christ is in me. Lord, I come now to Thee to set my heart open before Jesus, and to receive Him as my Saviour. Amen.

Prayer

(for one who has discovered that Jesus Christ is not in him)

Lord God, I had thought of going forward to Thy table. A sense of obligation came even to me, and I made myself ready for the hour of the feast. But, behold, Thy Word has made me afraid. It tells me that, if Jesus Christ is not in me, I am reprobate.

Lord, have compassion upon me. I know that I may not sit down without the wedding garment. Thou art the Lord of table; Thy Word must prevail there. Thou art the Holy God. Thou canst not meet in love with the sinner who is not washed from his sin and clothed with the righteousness of Christ. And, Lord, I fear that I am still without that wedding garment: my sins are not forgiven me. Lord, have pity upon me: I dare not go to Thy table: the bread of the children is not for me.

I dare not go forward. And yet, Lord, I dare not remain away. To have no part in Jesus, no share in Thy friendship, no place in the Marriage Supper of the Lamb on high—woe is me, if this must be my lot. Lord, have mercy upon me, and, if it be possible, grant unto me that which I require for sitting down at Thy table.

Wednesday Morning - Self Examination

Lord God, I have heard of Thy mercy. Thou givest the wedding garment for nothing: Thou forgivest the vilest sinner. Too long have I been content without really having Jesus Christ in me. Lord, now I come to Thee. Before Thee I lay my unrighteousness, which is great. I am entirely under the power of sin, and cannot help myself. Lord, Thou alone canst help me: and Thou wilt also do it. Be pleased to receive me. I cast myself down here before Thee: I here surrender myself to Thee. This day let the blood of Jesus wash me.

Lord Jesus, given by the Father for me, I receive Thee. I receive Thee, Lord, as my Saviour. I believe that Thou art for me. Here I give Thee my heart—my poor, sinful heart: come and dwell in it, and let me also know that Jesus Christ is in me.

My God, my soul cries out and longs for Thee: make me truly partaker of Jesus. Amen.

My Prayer for Today:

My Prayer for Today:

Thursday Morning

Thursday Morning
Confession of Sin

"I will declare mine iniquity; I will be sorry for my sin." "How many are mine iniquities and sins: make me to know my transgression and my sin." " Blessed are they that mourn, for they shall be comforted." —Psalm 38:18 Job 8; 23; Matthew 5:4.

"At the outset" says our Directory, "let everyone examine his heart, to see whether he be grieved on account of his sins, and humble himself before God." This is the first element of genuine self-examination. It cannot indeed be otherwise. The salvation of the Lord Jesus is a salvation from sin. The power, the grace, the Blessing of Jesus are exhibited in the taking away of sin out of us, and the implanting within us instead of the holiness and the life of Heaven. And it is because the Lord's Supper is intended to serve as a renewed and an increased participation of the life of Christ, that a new and deeper acknowledgment of sin is the most desirable preparation for the Supper. It is not merely he that is still seeking for forgiveness who must think of and confess his sins. No: it is especially the believer that has need to acknowledge aright and with all earnestness the sins which he still commits and their antipathy to God. The more he really despairs of himself, the more glorious will Christ become in his eyes. The more keenly he feels every sin, the more will Jesus become to him. Every sin is a need that calls for Jesus. By the confession of sin, you point out to Him the spot where you are wounded, and where He must exhibit the healing power of His blood. Every sin that you confess is an acknowledgment of something which Jesus must cast out, and the place of which He is bound to fill up with one of the lovely gifts of His holiness. Every sin that you confess is a new reason why you should believe more and ask more, and a new reason why Jesus should bless you.

Christian, prepare yourself for the Holy Supper by thinking of your sins. Be not afraid to make mention of them by name before Jesus. Point out to Him that which you desire He should change in you. Sin which is not confessed is also not combated. When a saved soul goes to Jesus to speak with Him about sin, and to make it known to Him, it breaks sin's power and makes Him more precious. The very same light that enables you to feel the curse of sin more deeply, enables you also to discern the perfect and final victory over it. The experience, *utterly lost,* prepares the way for the experience *utterly redeemed.*

Beloved child of God, you do not perhaps yet know what a source of blessing a deep conviction of sin is. Do not be afraid of it: do not turn away from it. The blessed Spirit of God will give it to you. Through the increasing grace of Jesus in you, through your deepening fellowship in the life of Heaven, He will so discover its incurable sinfulness, that this very experience shall lead you to that entire surrender to Jesus which is so gloriously sealed in the Lord's Supper.

Prayer

Lord God, Thou searchest and knowest us. Thou art He that knowest the hearts and triest the reins. Before Thee, there is no creature that is not made manifest: but all things are naked and open before the eyes of Him with whom we have to do. Thine eyes see through the heart alike of the ungodly and the righteous. Thou art the Omniscient One, the Searcher of hearts.

Lord, how terrible is Thine omniscience for Thine enemies. That eye which burns in heaven as a flame of fire is always upon them. They would fain flee away from it, but they are never able. But for Thy people, Thine omniscience is a comfort and a refuge. Thou art He who can help them against themselves and the deceitfulness of their own hearts. They invite Thine omniscience to search their heart and to cleanse them from their secret faults.

Holy God, I too place myself in Thine hands. Search *me*, O God, and know my heart. With fear, and yet from the depths of my heart, I say unto thee: Holy God, I wish to tolerate no single sin, however secret or deeply rooted it may be. Lord, I crave Thy help: I place myself in the light of Thy flaming eyes, before which no sin can stand. Search me, O God, and know my heart.

Thursday Morning - Confession of Sin

I Know, Lord, that the answer is often times terrible: "By terrible things Thou wilt answer us in righteousness, O God of our salvation." I know, when Thou dost suffer man to enter into temptation and let him see what is in his heart, that the humiliation and the shame and the sorrow are often deep and bitter. I know that when Thou trustest Thy mighty hand into the bosom to root out the almost unknown and yet deeply-rooted sin, flesh and blood must then fail. And yet I cry: Search me, O God, and know my heart.

Lord, make me know the sin to which I am blind: my characteristic sins also, about which I am so sensitive when any other speaks of them, whether it be the love of money with its seduction, or the love of the world with its vanity, or the love of self with its entanglement, make me to know it. Lord, use friend or foe: use what means Thou wilt, O my Father: only search me and know my heart: cleanse me from secret errors, and let no hurtful way abide with me, but lead me in the way that is everlasting.

Yes, gracious Lord, give me such an overmastering conviction of the entire corruption of my nature that I shall be constrained to receive in its completeness the perfect redemption of Christ. Amen.

My Prayer for Today:

Friday Morning

Friday Morning
Faith

"Thy sins are forgiven. Thy faith hath saved thee: go in peace."—LUKE 7:48-50.

At the table Jesus gathers His friends, and the Father waits only for His children to distribute to them the children's bread. The table is not the place for me to be converted or to ask the expiation of my sins. No: these blessings I must seek in solitude: in the inner chamber Jesus will suffer Himself to be found with eagerness and certainty. The table is the place for His redeemed to confess their Lord, for His believers to have their faith strengthened, for His friends to renew their covenant. On this account our Directory mentions to us as the second element of self-examination before we go to the table, the question whether we really believe in the forgiveness of sins. "In the next place, let everyone examine his heart as to whether be also believes this sure promise of God that all his sins are forgiven for Christ's sake." It is through faith in the forgiveness of sins that the soul obtains confidence to draw near to the Lord, and thereby also obtains the blessing of a strengthened faith.

Reader, you are to go to the Lord's Supper: do you believe in the forgiveness of your sins? You know what this means. Forgiveness is not the taking away of the sinfulness of the heart or sanctification: no, but only the beginning of the way by which it is to be reached. Forgiveness is the free declaration by which God acquits you of the evil you have hitherto done, and no longer reckons the guilt of it to you. Forgiveness comes first in order: then forthwith begins sanctification and renewal. For the present this is the question before you: Do you believe in the forgiveness of your sins—that your sins are blotted out?

You know what faith is. You know that it is a feeling, an experience of something that keeps man intently occupied with his own condition. You know that it is a going out of ourselves to find a resting place in God and His Word, so that faith in the forgiveness of sins is the certitude that your sins are forgiven, and that on no other ground except that God has said He has done so. Consequently, faith that your sins are forgiven is nothing but the confidence that you, as a poor sinner resting in His Word, have come to Him, and that your sins have been blotted out of His book. You know it, because God has promised it.

Reader, do you thus believe in the forgiveness of sins—"that your sins are blotted out for Christ's sake"? Are you one of those concerning whom the Directory says: "Let everyone examine his heart whether he has believed the sure promise of God that all his sins are forgiven, and that the perfect righteousness of Christ is bestowed upon him and reckoned to him as his own"? Yea, as completely as if he himself in his own person had atoned for all his sins and fulfilled all righteousness.

Blessed are ye who believe this. You have confidence to draw near to the Lord's Table. Believing in the truth of the word, "He abundantly pardons," believing in the power of Jesus Christ really to cleanse the conscience, believing with a personal appreciation that the promise of forgiveness is also for you, you know that your guilt is blotted out—that your sins are remembered no more.

Christian, come to the table in this faith. Let your song of praise be: "Bless the Lord, O my soul, who forgiveth all thine iniquities." Ask for the Holy Spirit, that He may make faith in forgiveness within you more certain, more powerful, more joyful. You will then experience at the table what a life of love and blessing and growing power God has prepared for all on whom He first bestows the forgiveness of sins.

Prayer

Lord God, I find myself on the way to Thy table. I desire also to receive there what Jesus gives when He says: "This cup is the New Covenant in My blood which is poured out for you *for the forgiveness of sins.*" Lord, I desire this day to acknowledge in a new act of faith my participation in the forgiveness of sins, and thus to meet with Thee at the Supper as Thine own in the joy of redemption.

For this end, wilt Thou grant unto me a sight of the work of Jesus as all-sufficient and perfectly fulfilled, so that there is nothing for me now to do save to receive it and rejoice in it? Renew in me by the Holy Spirit the living assurance of my part in Jesus. And help me, Lord, with a clearer faith than ever before to appropriate the whole redemption of Thy Son with all Thy rich and glorious promises.

Lord, I beseech Thee, let no doubt rob me of this blessing. When I look to myself, there is nothing but fear, and condemnation. When I have to question my heart and what I feel there, I have no hope. But I look to Thy Word. It makes me cry out: *"Who is a God like unto Thee that forgiveth iniquity?"* (Mic. 7:18). That Word points me to the Cross of Thy dear Son, who died for the ungodly, and says to me: "The blood of Jesus Christ cleanseth from all sin." "If we confess our sins, He is faithful and *righteous* to forgive all our sins." That Word teaches me to say: "With Thee is forgiveness." Lord, on that Word I depend: With Thee is forgiveness. I have confessed my sin before Thee: I lay my whole sinfulness bare before Thee, and I believe that through the virtue of the blood of Jesus, Thou forgivest my sin.

My God, grant me grace to hold fast by this truth, and with every fresh sin to flee always straight to the blood of Christ. Grant that I may sit down at Thy table with the blessed joy of a firm faith in the great promise of the New Covenant: "I will be gracious to your iniquities, and your sins and transgressions will I remember no more."

Lord God, this Thou hast said, and that *will I believe.* Amen.

My Prayer for Today:

My Prayer for Today:

Saturday Morning

Saturday Morning
Self-Surrender

"The love of Christ constraineth us; because we thus judge that one died for all, therefore all died: and He died for all, that they which live shall no longer live unto themselves, but unto Him who for their sake died, and rose again."

—2 Cor. 5:14-15.

"In the third place, let everyone examine his heart to see whether He is conscious of having heretofore manifested genuine thankfulness toward God with his whole life." So the Directory expresses what Must Constitute the third part of self-examination, whether I have been hitherto conscious of dedicating myself to the Lord as a living thank offering, not in single things only, but in my whole life.

This is what Jesus desires. Every redeemed soul must be a man consecrated to God, entirely separated to live for Him, His will, His work, His honor. This also is what the true Christian desires: he acknowledges the equity of the demand which Jesus makes, the perfect right which Jesus has to him as His blood-bought possession. This is what the true Christian expects in the power of the love of Christ shed abroad in the heart, in the strength of the new life. And this dedication, this complete surrender, is what the believer especially confesses and completes in the Lord's Supper.

The Lord's Supper is always a sacrificial repast, and that in a double sense. Under the Old Covenant there were special sacrifices—namely, the sin offering, the burnt offering, and the thank offering. The sin offering, by which atonement was made, was the type of the sacrifice of Christ alone. "He was made sin for us." The burnt offering, which had to be wholly consumed by fire on the altar, as a symbol of entire devotedness to the service of God, was the type alike of the sacrifice of Christ and of the sacrifice of believers in which they surrender themselves to the Lord (Rom. 12:1). Then last, the idea of thank offering is exhibited more fully to the apprehension in the feast of thank offering and in the fellowship that ensued.

Of the sin offering, by which atonement was made, the priests might eat, as a token of their fellowship with God through the atonement. The Lord's Supper is our fellowship in the perfect sacrifice of Jesus Christ which has done away with sin forever. Of the thank offering in which dedication to God was shown forth, the offerer himself might also eat in recognition of his fellowship with God in this dedication. The Lord's Supper is a communion with Christ, not only because He offered Himself up for us, but because in and with Him we offer ourselves to the Father with all that we have.

Marvelous union: Jesus offers Himself to me: I offer myself to Him: Jesus gives Himself wholly for me: I give myself wholly for Him. My sacrifice is the counterpart, the reflection, of His.

With what earnestness did He prepare Himself for the fulfillment of His sacrifice, in order that His will might really yield itself completely and wholly to the Father. As for me, how much more need have I of preparation for asking whether, while I take a whole Christ for myself, I yield myself with my whole life to Him.

"Let every one examine his heart." Believer, the observance of the Supper is a glorious opportunity of renewed dedication to your Lord. Let the Holy Spirit discover to you what it is to be a decided Christian: undividingly, unceasingly surrendered to Jesus in heart and hand and lips, at home and in society; living for Jesus, working zealously for Jesus; a burnt offering which is given entirely for God, and is consumed by the fire of the Spirit. In this spirit, prepare yourself to be willingly bound to the horns of the altar.

PRAYER

My Father, Thou callest me to Thy table to participate by faith anew in the sacrifice of Thy Son: I cry to Thee, in turn, to make me partaker of the power, the inclination, and the spirit of His self-sacrifice, that I, in fellowship with Him, may in like manner offer myself up to Thee. "Through the Eternal Spirit He offered Himself up to God." My God, let the same Spirit make me also, on my part, a complete offering to Thee.

My Father, grant unto me to see that self-offering constitutes the essence and the worth of His sacrifice. Let the surrender of my feeling and will to the will of God be the mark of my piety. Yea, Lord, let me live as one who offers himself wholly to the desire of God and man to further Thine honor and their salvation.

My Father, at the Supper I desire truly to present myself as a living, holy sacrifice, well pleasing, to God—an offering that shall be wholly consumed.

For this end I entreat Thee for grace to prepare myself for this sacrifice, as Thy Son prepared Himself for the sacrifice on Golgotha by saying in Gethsemane: "Not My will, but Thine be done. So would I offer myself as a sacrifice to Thee with the complete surrender of my will: may Thy will be all in all to me, O my God. Lord enable me to say in truth: 'I live only to do the will of God.' In the strength of Jesus Christ, who liveth in me and in whom I offer myself to Thee, I venture to make His language my own: 'Lo I come to do Thy will, O God!'

Lord, prepare me also to say: I desire here before Thee to renounce every known and unknown sin. All self-seeking and self-will I desire to abandon before Thee. I take Jesus Christ as my holiness, my strength, my victory; and in virtue of the new nature which He has prepared for me, I say: Father, no more sin, but Thy will only—Thy will wholly, Thy will always and in all.

Lord Jesus, who didst give Thyself for me, I give myself to Thee. Yea, Lord, in this very moment, where I in solitude am this morning preparing myself for the Supper, I say before Heaven and earth: Jesus, Son of God, I will give myself wholly to Thee, to live now and henceforth only for Thee. Lord Jesus, I do this now. And as one who is offered to the Father and to Thee, I will go to the Supper table, there to be confirmed in the faith and confession; I am no longer my own I have been bought with a high price: I will glorify God in my body and my spirit, which are God's.

My Prayer for Today:

Saturday Evening

Saturday Evening
A Prayer for the Holy Spirit

Lord God, I thank Thee heartily that Thou hast led me throughout this week of preparation, and that I can now cherish the hope of eating with Thee and Thy Son on the morrow at the Table of the Covenant. I thank Thee for every opportunity of meditation and prayer, so that I may not thoughtlessly appear in the sanctuary. In this quiet evening hour, I come once more to Thee to beseech Thee for the gift of the Holy Spirit.

Lord God, Thou hast taught us to say that without Him there can be no true prayer, no real fellowship with Thyself. Therefore hast Thou given to every one of Thy children the Holy Spirit, by whom they may have access in Christ to the Father. Lord, what I would entreat of Thee is this: that the Spirit may now work mightily in me, so as to impart to me all the dispositions by which I may draw near to Thee in the holy adornment of Thy chosen ones. I know that I have only been all too unfaithful to Him. Father, forgive me, and take not Thy Holy Spirit from me.

May He convince me anew of sin. May He work in me true penitence, so that I may remember my sinfulness with a contrite heart. O Lord, my God, I desire this evening to remember, to confess, and to cast away every sin that still cleaves to me. (Here the believing suppliant may think of his own special sins, confess them, and abjure them before God.) I would think with loathing on myself and the deep aversion of my nature from God, and would forever renounce all confidence in myself, and all satisfaction with myself. Lord God, let the Holy Spirit so work in me, and spiritually so renew me, that all sin shall become more and more hateful and intolerable; and that in like manner, through the spiritual acknowledgement of my corrupt nature, I may meet with Thee in a more humble and tender spirit. May a sweet, blessed lowliness of mind be the fruit of a rich indwelling of the Spirit in my heart.

Saturday Evening - A Prayer for the Holy Spirit

And Lord, in like manner may the result of Thine own Spirit's operation in me be a strong, a joyful faith, that a full Christ, with all His promises and all His blessings, is inwardly appropriated and enjoyed. Yea, my God, may the Spirit bring out in me that fruit which in the sight of man seems so undesirable—the humility of one who feels himself worthy only of rejection, coupled with the gladness of one who is redeemed, who is a beloved child.

May He also discover to me, and shed abroad in me, the eternal love of our God, so that my experience of His personal affection for me may be a thousandfold clearer and more certain than the affection of any man on earth. O Lord, the Holy Spirit can effect this. He can bring down from heaven into my soul the love of God as a real gift: grant that this gift may be near at this time of communion. Lord, I depend upon Thy promise; I wait for the mighty working of the Spirit.

Then shall my love burst out into a flame at the Table. Then shall I behold the countenance of my Lord, and my whole heart shall be won by Him. Then shall my surrender to the Lord be a real and effectual one. Blessed God, withhold not from me, but bestow on me in large measure, the mighty operations of Thy Holy Spirit. Thou hast given Him to be in me: may He now fill me. Then shall my observance of the Supper be truly a fellowship of the Spirit with the Father and the Son. Then shall I have not only heavenly blessing around me and in me, but also heavenly life in me, both to know and to receive all His blessing.

Lord, I depend upon Thy promises: I set myself now in silence before Thee to wait for the Spirit: I give myself to Him in the faith that He will work in me. I ask this One boon besides: that in Thy servant who presides over the congregation, and in the congregation itself, Thy blessed Spirit, with His silent heavenly power, may be mightily at work, so that this festal time may be for all a time of great blessing. Would that some who are still dead may now be made alive.

Lord, grant this for the sake of Thy Son. Amen.

My Prayer for Today:

Part II

The Communion Sabbath

The Lord's Table

Here, O my Lord, I see Thee face to face;
Here would I touch and handle things unseen;
Here grasp with firmer hand and eternal grace
And all my weariness upon Thee lean.

Here would I feed upon the bread of God,
Here drink with Thee the royal wine of Heaven;
Here would I lay aside each earthly load,
Here taste afresh the calm of sin forgiven.

This is the hour of banquet and of song;
This is the Heavenly table spread for me;
Here let me feast, and feasting still prolong
The brief, bright hour of fellowship with Thee.

—Horatius Bonar

THE MORNING OF THE LORD'S DAY

An Exercise of Faith

Beloved Lord Jesus, to Thee is the desire of my soul. Thou art He in whom the love of the Father is disclosed to me. Thou art He who hast loved me even unto death on earth, and still lovest me in Thy glory on high. Thou art He in whom alone my soul has its life. Beloved Lord Jesus, my soul cleaves hard to Thee. On this holy morning I will prepare myself to go to the table by exercising and confessing anew my faith in Thee. My Saviour, do Thou Thyself come into me: my faith can only be the fruit of what Thou givest me to know of Thyself.

My Saviour, I come to Thee this morning, as aforetime, with the confession that there is nothing in myself on which I can lean. All my experiences confirm to me what Thou hast said of my corruption: that in me, that is, in my flesh, there dwelleth no good thing. And yet I come to Thee to lay my claim before Thee, to let it prevail with Thee, and to take Thee as mine own. O, my

Lord, my claim rests on the Word of my Father, that He has given His Son for sinners, that Thou didst die for the ungodly. My sinfulness is my claim upon Thee: Thou art for sinners. My claim is God's eternal righteousness: the Surety has paid; the guilty must go free. My claim rests on Thy love: Thou hast compassion on the wretched. My claim is Thy faithfulness: O, my Saviour, I have given myself to Thee and Thou hast received me, and what Thou hast begun in me, Thou wilt gloriously complete. That which has passed betwixt Thee and me gives me increased courage; and now I come to take Thee as mine, and enjoy Thee, with all Thou art and hast. Blessed Lord, unveil Thyself to me, in order that my faith may be truly strong and joyful.

Yes: Lord Jesus, Thou art mine: with all Thy fulness Thou art mine. God be praised, I can say this: Thy blood is mine: it has atoned for all, yea all, my sins. Thy righteousness is mine; yea, Thou Thyself art my righteousness, and makest me altogether acceptable to the Father. Thy love is mine: yea, in all its height and depth and length and breadth is Thy love mine, O Jesus: it is the habitation in which I abide, the very air I breathe. And all that Thou hast is mine. Thy wisdom is mine; Thy strength is mine; Thy holiness is mine; Thy life is mine; Thy glory is mine; Thy Father is mine. Beloved Lord Jesus, my soul has only one desire this day: that Thou, my Almighty Friend, wouldst make me with a silent but very powerful activity of faith to behold Thee, and inwardly appropriate

Thee as my possession. Lord Jesus, in the simplicity of faith that depends only on Thee, I say: God be praised, Jesus with all His fulness is mine. How little do I yet thoroughly know or enjoy this truth: Jesus with all His fulness is mine.

Help me now, Lord, to go to Thy table in the blessed expectation of new communications out of the treasures of Thy love. Let my faith be not only strong, but large: may it cause me to open my mouth wide.

I have so much of which I stand in need today. But what I need above all is this: that I may know my Lord as the daily food of my soul, and that I may comprehend how He will every day be my strength and my life. My desire is that I may understand that not only at the Lord's Supper, but every hour of my life on earth, my Lord Jesus is willing to take the responsibility of my life, to be my life, and to live His life in me. O Jesus, do enable me to grasp this truth today.

Beloved Lord, I believe that Thou hast the power to work this in me. I know that Thy love is waiting for me, and will take great delight in doing this for me. I believe, Lord, and Thou wilt come to help my unbelief. Yea, although I do not as yet thoroughly understand it, I will believe that my Jesus will this day communicate Himself anew to me as my life, and wilt give me, through the operation of His Holy Spirit, a larger participation of His heavenly life which He lives on high. I will believe that what He this day does, He will every day henceforth confirm. Yea, my precious Saviour, I will this day betake me with all my misery, and make myself over to Thee to dwell in me. And I will believe that Thou, because Thou art wholly my possession, wilt make myself ready and come in and take possession of me, and fill me with Thyself. Lord, I believe: increase this faith within me.

And now, Lord, prepare me and all Thy congregation for a blessed observance of the Supper. Now, unto Him that is able to do exceeding abundantly above all that we ask or think, according to the power that worketh in us, unto Him be the glory in the Church and in Christ Jesus, unto all generations forever and ever. Amen.

My Prayer for Today:

1
Take Eat

"Take, eat; this is My body which is given for you." — Matthew 26:26; Luke 22:19.

When the Lord says this, He points out to us that His body is not so much *His* as it is *ours*, since He received it and suffered it to be broken on the cross, not for His own sake, but for ours; and that He now also desires that we should look upon it and appropriate it as our own possession. Thus, with His body, He gives Himself to us, and desires that we should take Him. The fellowship of the Lord's Supper is a fellowship of giving and taking. Blessed giving: blessed taking.

Blessed giving: the person gives value to the gift. Who is He that gives? It is my Creator, who comes here to give what my soul needs. It is my Redeemer, who, at the table, will give to me in possession what He has purchased for me.

And what gives He? His body and His blood. He gives the greatest and the best He can bestow: yea, all that it is possible for Him to give—the broken body which He first offered to the Father as a sacrifice for sin, a sacrifice that filled Him with joy. And what He offered to the Father, to put away sin before Him, He now offers to me, to put away sin in me.

And wherefore gives He this? Because He loves me. He desires to redeem me from death, and to bestow on me eternal life in Himself. He gives Himself to me to be the food, the joy, the living power of my soul. O blessed, Heavenly giving of eternal love! Jesus gives me His own body: Jesus gives me Himself.

And not less *blessed taking*, for it is so simple. Just as I receive with my hand the bread that is intended for me, and hold it before me as my own, so by faith in the word, in which Jesus gives Himself to me, I take Him for myself, and I know that He is really mine. The body in which He suffered for sin is my possession: the power of His atonement is mine. The body of Jesus is my food and my life.

And how *free* is the taking. I think of my unworthiness, only to find in it my claim on Him, the Righteous One, who died for the unrighteous. I think of my misery only as the poverty and the hunger for which the festal repast is prepared, this divine bread so cordially given.

Take Eat

What Jesus in His love would give so heartily and willingly, I will as heartily and freely take.

And so real is the taking. Where God gives, there is power and life. In giving, there is a communication, a real participation of that which is bestowed. Consequently, my taking does not depend on my strength: I have only to receive what my Saviour brings to me and inwardly imparts. I, a mere worm, take what He, the Almighty, gives. Blessed giving, blessed taking.

Blessed God, may my taking be in conformity with Thy giving; Thy giving, the standard and the measure of my taking. What God gives, I take as a whole. As Thou givest, so I also receive, —heartily, undividedly, lovingly. Precious Saviour, my taking depends wholly on Thy giving.

Come Thou and give: give Thyself truly and with power in the communion of the Spirit. Come, my eternal Redeemer, and let Thy love delight itself and be satisfied in me, whilst Thou dost unfold to me the divine secret of the word: My body *given* for you. Yea, Lord, I wait upon Thee. What thou givest me as my share in Thy broken body, that will I take and eat. And my soul shall go hence, joyful and strengthened, to thank Thee and to serve Thee. Amen.

My Prayer for Today:

2
In Remembrance of Me

"Do this in remembrance of Me."—Luke 22:19

" Do this in remembrance of me." Is this injunction, then, really necessary? Can it be possible that I should forget Jesus?

Forget Jesus! Jesus, who thought of me in eternity; who, indeed, forgot His own sorrows on the Cross, but never forgets mine; who says to me that a mother will sooner forget her sucking child than He in Heaven will forget me. Can I forget Jesus? Jesus, my Sun, my Surety, my Bridegroom; my Jesus, without whose love I cannot live: can I ever forget Jesus?

Ah, me! how often have I forgotten Jesus. How frequently has my foolish heart grieved Him and prepared all manner of sorrow for itself by forgetting Jesus. At one time it was in the hour of care, or sin, or grief, at another in prosperity and joy, that I suffered myself to be led astray. O my soul, be deeply ashamed that Thou shouldst ever forget Jesus.

And Jesus will not be forgotten. He will see to it that this shall not take place for His own sake. He loves us so dearly that He sets great store by our love, and cannot endure to be forgotten. Our love is to Him His happiness and joy: He requires it from us with a holy strictness: He cannot endure to be forgotten. So truly has the eternal Love chosen us that it longs to live in our remembrance every day.

For our sakes also He will see to it that He is not forgotten. By the memory, through this kind of remembrance, the past becomes the present in perspective. Jesus always yearns to be with us and beside us, that He may make us taste of His crucified love and the power of His heavenly life. Jesus wills that we should always remember Him.

How I long never more to forget Jesus. Thank God, Jesus will so give Himself to me at the table that He shall become to me one never to be forgotten. At the table He will overshadow and satisfy me with His love. He will make His love to me so glorious that my love shall always hold Him in remembrance. What is more, He will so unite Himself with me, will so give His life in me, that out of the power of His own indwelling in me it will not be possible for me to forget Him. I have too much considered it a duty and a work to remember Jesus. Lord Jesus, so fill me with Thy joy that it will be an impossibility for me not to remember Thee.

Jesus remembers me with such a tender love that He desires and will grant that the remembrance of Him shall always live in me. It is for this end that He gives me the new remembrance of His love in the Lord's Supper. I will draw near to it in this joyful assurance: Jesus will there teach me to remember Him always.

My Lord, how wonderful is this Thy love: that it should be a matter of deep interest to Thee to be Held in remembrance by us, and that Thou shouldst always desire to live in our remembrance in our love. Thou knowest, Lord, that it is not by any force my heart can be taught to remember Thee. But if by Thy love Thou dwellest in me, thinking of Thee becomes a joy, —no effort or trouble, but the sweetest rest. Lord, my soul praises Thee for the wonderful grace of the Supper. First, Thou givest Thyself in Thine eternal and unchangeable love as the daily food of our souls, and then Thou dost charge us, out of the power of Thy promised presence, wherewith Thou wilt feed us, not to forget Thee. Now I dare promise it. O my Lord, at Thy table, give Thou Thyself to my soul as its food, be every day my food, and Thy love shall keep the thought of Thee ever living. Then shall I never forget Thee; no, not for a single moment. For then I shall have no life save in Thy love. Amen.

My Prayer for Today:

3
My Blood

"And He took a cup, and gave thanks, and gave to them, saying, Drink ye all of it; for this is My blood." "The cup of blessing which we bless, is it not a communion of the blood of Christ?"—Matthew 26:27, 28; 1 Corinthians 10:16.

"For the life of the flesh is in the blood: and I have given it to you upon the altar to make atonement for your souls: for it is the blood that maketh atonement by reason of the life" (Leviticus 27:11). For the blood is the life, the living spirit; and therefore atonement is linked with the shedding of blood. It was the surrender of the life of an innocent animal in the place of guilty man. And thus with the shedding of Jesus' blood, His life is surrendered for our sins. The worth and the power of that blood are the worth and the power of the life of Jesus. Every drop of that blood has in it the power of an endless life.

Jesus gives me His blood. When I become partaker of that blood, I have part in the atonement which it established, the forgiveness which it secured. I have part in all that wonderful suffering in which it was shed. I have part in all the love of which that suffering and that bloodshedding were the revelation. I have part in that life which is in the blood and is in it first surrendered and then taken up again. I have part in the life of Jesus, surrendered upon the Cross, raised from the grave and now glorified in Heaven. O glorious wonders of grace which lie hid in that Word: "Drink, for this is My blood."

The blood of Jesus is my drink of life. Jesus' love is the power of my life. The spirit of Jesus' life is the spirit of my life. O my God, help me to conceive these wonders. How powerful, how heavenly must that life be which is nourished by the New Wine of the kingdom and has communion with the blood of God's Son, not only by cleansing, but also by drinking.

Blessed Jesus, who hast loved me so wonderfully, Thou wilt not deny me the request which I now state to Thee: unfold to me the secret of Thy life in me which Thou bestowest upon me, when from above Thou still givest me to drink the blood shed for the forgiveness of my sins. Most precious Saviour, illumine and enlarge my faith, that I may now realize this truth: Jesus' own life is in my innermost being, the life of my life. He "through His own blood entered in once for all into the holy place, having obtained eternal redemption" with the Father. Through Thine own blood come Thou to my heart to bring in this redemption there also. Lord Jesus, my heart thirsts for Thee. Come this day to me with that precious blood and let the full power of it be unveiled to me by Thyself. Let it quench my thirst. Let it cleanse me from all unrighteousness. Let it bring me into harmony with the joy and praise of those who sing: "Unto Him that loveth us and loosed us from our sins by His blood, to Him be the glory and the dominion forever." Amen.

My Prayer for Today:

4
The New Covenant

"And the cup in like manner after supper, saying, This cup is the new covenant in My blood."—Luke 22:20.

The Lord's Supper is a covenant meal—the Feast of the New Covenant. It is of great importance to understand the New Covenant thoroughly.

It is something quite different from the Old Covenant—infinitely better and more glorious. The Old Covenant which God made with Israel was indeed glorious, but yet not adapted for sinful man, because he could not fulfill it. God gave to His people His perfect law, with the glorious promises of His help, His guidance, His blessing, if they should continue in the observance of it. But man in his inner life was still under the power of sin: he was lacking in the strength requisite for abiding in the covenant of His God.

God promised to make a New Covenant. *(Read with care Jeremiah 31:31-34, 33:38-42; Hebrews 8:6-14.)* In this

New Covenant, God promised to bestow the most complete forgiveness of sins and to take man altogether into His favor. He further promised to communicate to him His law, not externally as written on tables, but inwardly and in his heart, so that he should have strength to fulfill its precepts. He was to give him a new heart and a new spirit—in truth, His own Holy Spirit. Man was not called on in the first instance to promise that he would walk in God's law. God rather took the initiative in promising that He would enable him to do so. *"I will put My Spirit within you,"* said the Lord by Ezekiel (36:27), *"and cause you to walk in My statutes, and ye shall keep My judgments and do them."*

Of this New Covenant, Jesus is the Mediator and Surety (Heb. 12:22, 8:6). As Surety, He stands pledged to us to secure that God will fulfill all His promises. As Surety, He is no less pledged to God in our behalf that we shall keep God's commandments. Glorious covenant of grace, with its wonderful provision for all our needs. In the Lord Jesus, God saw it meet to establish this covenant, without fear that His rights would suffer any violation. God could rely upon His Son to see to it that His honor should be respected. And in Jesus I also may well dare to enter into this covenant, without fear that I shall not be able to fulfill it: I can rely upon Jesus to see to it that He will bring everything to completion for and in me. In the New Covenant, Jesus the Surety has not only wholly discharged the old debt, but also undertaken the responsibility for whatever else may be still required in our case.

In this New Covenant, I this day surrender myself to Thee, O my God. Thou wilt bind me to Thyself with Thy glorious promises. Thou bindest Thyself to forgive my sins, to love me as Thy child, to train, to sanctify, to bless me; to give me light, and desire, and strength for abiding in Thy covenant and doing Thy will. And I am bound to Thee in Thy precious Son. Eternal God, grant that the Holy Spirit, who is one of the promises of this New Covenant, may this day unfold to me what Thy love has destined for me in it. Wilt Thou make me to understand that Thou hast undertaken and promised to secure that I shall walk in Thy ways, and that Thou givest me Thy Son as the Surety of the Covenant to carry out all its details? Then shall I take Thy Son and the Covenant sealed with His blood, with the blessed joy of knowing that He will be in me the fulfilling of the covenant, the fulfilling as well of Thy covenant promises as of my covenant obligations.

Blessed Jesus, reach to me this day *the blood of the covenant.* Amen.

My Prayer for Today:

5
Unto Remission of Sins

"My blood, which is shed unto remission of sins." — Matthew 26:28.

Sin: at the Lord's Table, this word is not to be dispensed with. It is sin that gives us a right to Christ. It is as a Saviour from sin that Christ desires to have to do with us. It is as sinners that we sit down at the table. If I cannot always come immediately to Christ and appropriate Him, I can always come on the ground of my sin. Sin is the handle by which I can take hold of Christ. I may not always be able actually to lay my hand on Christ and say: *Christ is mine*; but I can always say: *Sin is mine.* And when I then hear the glad tidings that Christ died for sin, I obtain courage to say: *Sin is mine,* and Christ, who died for sin, died also for me. When I look upon my own righteousness, I have no courage: but when I first look on sin, I can make bold to say that Christ is mine. *Sin*: how sweet it is to me to hear that word from the *mouth* of Jesus at the table.

And what does my Saviour say about sin? He speaks of it only to give the assurance of the forgiveness of sin. That God no more remembers my sin and does not impute it to me, that He does not desire to look upon my sin and deal with me in deserved wrath, but meets me in love and complacency as one whose sin is taken away: that is what my Jesus secures for me, where He points me to His blood and gives it to me as my own. And that is what thou mayest believe and enjoy, O my soul, when thou drinkest that blood. And when Thou askest Him to make known to thee by His Holy Spirit the divine glory of this forgiveness as complete, effectual, entire, always valid and eternal, then shalt thou, too, be able to sing: "Blessed is the man whose transgression is forgiven."

Then shall you also see how this forgiveness as a living seed includes in itself all other blessings. For to whom God forgives sin, him He also receives, him He loves, him He acknowledges as a child, and gives him the Holy Spirit with all His gifts. The forgiveness of sin is, as it were, the pledge of entrance into the whole riches of the grace of God. The soul that day by day really enjoys forgiveness in the Lord Jesus shall go hence in the joy and power of the Lord.

O what a blessed feast: to know myself to be one with Jesus as a ransomed soul, and, being in Him, to be able to look out upon my sin: this is true blessedness. Blessed it is, because there, while He points with His finger to the sin for which I must be so bitterly ashamed, I can hear this glorious word: "Forgiven." Blessed, because, for the confirmation of this forgiveness and the communication of all its blessing, I am there nourished by the very blood which was shed for remission of sins. Blessed, because in the joy of the forgiveness and the enjoyment of that blood, I am anew linked with that Jesus who loves me so wonderfully. Yea, blessed, because I know that in place of sins He now gives me Himself to fill my empty heart, in order that it be adorned with the light and the beauty of His own life. Blessed feast, blessed drinking unto remission of sins!

Precious Saviour, I am naturally so afraid to look upon my sins, to acknowledge, to combat them. In the joy and the power of Thy forgiveness, I dread this no more. Now I can look upon them as a victor. Help me to love Thee much, as one to whom much has been forgiven. Amen.

My Prayer for Today:

6
For Many

"My blood, which was shed for many."—Matthew 26:28

Jesus has a large heart. At the Supper Table, He not only forgot Himself, to think of His own who were gathered there around Him, but His loving eye glanced forward to all who are redeemed by His blood. "For Many": with this Word He teaches His disciples to maintain fellowship, not merely with those with whom they sit at the table, but with the entire host of the redeemed—the multitude that no man can number. In the light of this Word we see Him breaking, the bread and giving it to the disciples, and then again to the multitude after the day of Pentecost, and then yet again to others until the ever-widening circle extends to the spot where we now sit. This truth binds all cerebrations of the Supper into one single communion in immediate contact with Him who first instituted it. It unites also the separate circles of Christ's disciples into one universal Church, and all distinction and all separation vanish in the joyful thought that every member shares equally in the love and the life of the one Head from whom also He receives the bread. It sets the farthest distant in a relation to the love of Jesus as intimate as those who at the first received the broad from His own hand.

The observance of the Supper accordingly must renew our feeling of unity not only with the Head, but also with the Body of which we are members. The Supper must enlarge our heart, till it be as wide as the heart of Jesus. Next to love to the Lord Jesus must present love to the brethren fill our souls. Along with the word, "For you," which, as coming from His lips, is so precious to us, He desires us to couple and remember this other word, "For many."

"For many:" some Christians are satisfied when all goes well with their own little circle: they think of going to Heaven only in company with those that belong to them. This ought not to be. The Supper must enlarge the heart in love and prayer for all that belong to Jesus, so as to make us rejoice with them or weep with them. Nor even at this point must we stop. The true disciple of Jesus thinks of all who may yet be in their sin, and do not know about the blood which was shed "for many." Every real experience of the power of the blood must introduce me more deeply into the feelings and dispositions in which it was shed, and will constrain me to bring to the knowledge of it, the "many," for whom Christ poured it out. He that really drinks the blood which was shed "for many," and becomes inwardly partaker of the life and the love which was poured forth in that blood—how shall he find all selfishness and all narrow-mindedness vanishing, away, and have his heart enlarged to embrace the wide compass of Jesus' heart and Jesus' word, when He said: "My blood, shed for many."

Precious Saviour, grant unto me Thy Spirit, that the Same mind which is in Thee may be also in me. Cause me to understand how even of Thy holy Supper thou canst say: "Compel them to come in, that My house may be full." And may all Thy people be more filled with the thought: "Still there is room." O Lord Jesus, who Thyself art love, shed abroad Thy love in our hearts by Thy Holy Spirit. Amen.

My Prayer for Today:

7
For You

"My body, which is given for you. . . . My blood, which is shed for you."—Luke 22:19, 20.

It is an old saying: The whole secret of true blessedness lies in one word, the little word "Me." All knowledge of the truth, and all acquaintance with the gospel, are of no avail without the personal appropriation of that short phrase, For me. And that word of man has, on the other hand, its foundation in the word of Jesus, *"For you."*

So was it at the Lord's Table. In speaking of His body and blood, the Saviour addressed His disciples, and said to them: Given *for you*; shed *for you.*

How would the disciples in a later day feel themselves strengthened by that word. How could Peter in his deep fall, and Thomas in his grievous unbelief, and each of the others, fail to encourage themselves by remembering this: He spoke to me so cordially, just indeed as if it was meant for me alone, when He said: "Given for you."

It is in this word that for me also the richest blessing of the Lord's Supper is wrapt up. For, not less than to the first disciples, does the Saviour desire to say to every one of His guests: Given for you. By His Holy Spirit, He is as near to us as to them: He can make us feel the power of His eye and His voice. Not only by reaching the bread to each one separately, but much more by the heavenly operation of His Holy Spirit, will Jesus address each one, saying: *Given for you.*

Affecting word: how must it humble and subdue my heart. There sits the Son of God in His glory. There I bow myself in the dust, I who have been an enemy and ungodly, who am still all too much unfaithful and a transgressor. And, behold, with an eye in which holy earnestness is mingled with tender love, He points me to His broken body and shed blood, and says to me: For you, for you.

Lord, it is enough for that precious word my soul thanks Thee. That word I will lay hold of, and find in it confidence to return the answer: Yes, *for me, for me*; "for many," but yet also for me. The love, and the redemption, and the life, and the glory of which that blood speaks, I dare say of all: *For me, for me.*

Precious Jesus, my soul praises Thee for that loving word: For you. Hear my supplication, and let Thy Spirit at Thy table address it to me very powerfully. O strengthen me for a very confident and joyful appropriation of all that Thou sayest, and when my hand takes the bread, and I drink the wine, grant me with a very large and clear faith to say: *For me, for me.* Blessed Lord, I shall wait in silence for Thy Spirit; for to have that word from Thee is to me the secret of my blessing at the table. And Thou will give it to me. Amen.

My Prayer for Today:

My Prayer for Today:

8
One Body

"We who are many are one body: for we all partake of the one bread." "A new commandment I give unto you, that ye love one another; even as I have loved you, that ye also love one another. By this shall all men know that ye are my disciples, if ye have love one to another." —1 Corinthians 10:17; John 13:34, 35.

Union with the Lord Jesus, the Head, involves at the same time mutual union with the members of the body. He that really eats the body of Jesus and drinks His blood, is incorporated with His body, and stands thenceforth in the closest relationship to the whole body, with all its members. We have fellowship, not only in His body which He gave up to death, but especially in His body which He brought again from the dead—that is, the Church. "We are one body; for we all partake of the one bread."

So deep and wonderful was this union of His believing disciples at the table of the New Covenant, so entirely new the life of the Spirit by which they were to be gathered together into one in Him as His body, that the Lord spoke of the love which must animate them as a new commandment. In the New Covenant there was present a new life, and thus also a new love. "By this shall all men know that ye are My disciples, if ye have love one to another."

This thought is too much forgotten at the Lord's Table, and that to the great loss of the Church. How often have guests at Jesus' Table sat next [to] one another for years in concession without knowing or loving one another, without holding fellowship with one another, or helping one another. Many a one has sought after closer connection with the Lord and not found it, because they would have the Head alone without the body. Many a blessing has been missed and lost at the Supper, because the unity of the body was never considered. Yes: would that were it thoroughly understood; Jesus must be loved, and honored, and served, and known in His members. As by the circulation of the blood every member of our body is kept unceasingly in the most vital connection with the others, so the body of Christ can increase and become strong only when, in the loving interchange of the fellowship of the Spirit and of love, the life of the Head can flow unhindered from member to member. The observance of the Supper must be regarded as the conclusion of an alliance, not only with the Lord, but with all that sit at the table, to the effect that we shall live for one another. Not only must love to Him whose bread I eat be the object of desire, and promise, and prayer, but, also His love to all who eat that bread along with me there.

Blessed Lord, grant unto me to feel this truth aright. As really as in this bread which Thou dost impart to me, I maintain fellowship with Thee, I maintain it also with those with whom I share the bread at the table. As I receive Thee, so do I receive them. As I desire to confess, and love, and serve Thee, so would I also them. As I would be wholly one with Thee, so would I also with them. Very humbly do I acknowledge before Thee the sins of my old nature—selfishness, lovelessness, envy, wrath, indifference about others. Boldly and trustfully I entreat Thee for the love, the gentleness, the mercy, that are in Thee, to be shed abroad also in me. O Jesus, who givest Thyself to me, work in me and with me in all who eat of this one bread with me, Thine own heavenly love. Amen.

My Prayer for Today:

9
The Cup of Blessing

"The cup of blessing which we bless." —1 Corinthians 10:16.

[The Dutch version has: "The cup of thanksgiving which we bless with thanksgiving." —Translator]

The, Lord's Supper is properly a feast of thanksgiving. "When He had given thanks, He brake the bread." "In like manner He took the cup, and, when He had given thanks, He gave it to them." And after partaking of the Supper, it was "when they had sung an hymn," that they went out to the Mount of Olives. From Jewish writers, we also learn that the third cup of the Paschal feast, which was sanctified as the cup of the New Covenant, bore the name of the Cup of Thanksgiving, and that it was while it was being drunk that Psalms 116-118 were sung.

The Supper is a solemnity of redemption, the feast of the redeemed, a joyful repast at which God Himself says to us: "Let us eat and be merry"; a thanksgiving banquet at which is heard a prelude of the song of the Lamb. Let me ask grace to sit down joyfully and thankfully.

So shall I honor God. "He that offereth praise glorifieth Me." God is too little honored by His people. A joyful, thankful Christian shows that God can make those that serve Him truly happy. He stirs up others to praise God along with him.

So shall I enjoy the Supper aright. Sadness cannot eat; a joyful heart enjoys food. To be thankful for what I have received and for what my Lord has prepared, is the surest way to receive more.

So shall I be strengthened for conflict and for victory. "Thanks be to God, who always causeth us to triumph in Christ." "Thanks be to God, who giveth us the victory, through our Lord Jesus Christ." If my Saviour went singing from the Lord's Table to the conflict in Gethsemane, may I, in the joy of His redemption, follow Him with thanksgiving into every conflict to which He calls me.

So shall the Spirit of Heaven dwell in my heart. The nearer to the throne of God the more thanksgiving. This I see in the Revelation. In heaven they praise God day and night: a Lord's Supper pervaded by the spirit of thanksgiving is a foretaste of it.

And thou hast good cause to be thankful, soul. Look at Jesus, at His blood, at His redemption, at His love, at His blessed fellowship; and let all that is within thee praise Him. Drink, yea, drink abundantly, of the cup of thanksgiving, which we drink, giving thanks.

Blessed Lord, my Redeemer and my Friend, humbly I pray Thee: let my mouth be filled with Thy praise, all the day with Thy glory. Thou art in very truth our strength and song, for Thou hast become our salvation. Lord, teach me this day to take and drink the cup with thanksgiving, and to be joyful before Thy face. For this end, Thou hast only to unveil Thyself to me in the love that streams from Thy countenance, and the glorious redemption which Thou bringest, and my soul shall be suffused with joy. Is it not just for this end that thou didst institute the Supper? Precious Saviour, with thanksgiving shall I take the cup into my hand, in the blessed assurance that Thou wilt fill me with Thy love, my heart with Thy joy, my mouth with Thy praise. Praise the Lord, my soul, who satisfiest thy mouth with good things. Amen.

My Prayer for Today:

10
Till He Come

"Ye proclaim the Lord's death till He come." "I say unto you, I will not drink henceforth of this fruit of the vine until that day when I drink it new with you in My Father's kingdom." "I appoint unto you a kingdom, even as My Father appointed unto Me, that ye may eat and drink at My table in My kingdom."
—1 Corinthians 11:26; Matthew 26:29; Luke 22:29, 30.

At the Supper, Jesus points us not only backward, but also forward. From the suffering He points to the glory; out of the depths He calls to the heights. Because the Supper is the remembrance, the communion of Jesus, the living Saviour, it sets Him before us in all that He was, and is, and shall be. It is only in the future that we can expect to have the full realization of what is begun at the Lord's Supper. The Supper begins under the Cross with the reconciliation of the world; it is completed before the throne of glory in the new birth of the world. It is on this account that faith, according as it has experience of the power of the heavenly food, is irresistibly drawn on to the future. The true Christian has still to wait for his inheritance. "Till He come" is his watchword at every observance of the Supper. At the table his Lord speaks of drinking the fruit of the vine anew in the kingdom of the Father, and of eating and drinking at His table in His kingdom. The Supper, which is itself the fulfillment of the shadow of the Paschal Feast, is again in its turn the shadow of coming blessings, the pledge of the time when they shall cry: "Blessed are they that are called to the marriage Supper of the Lamb."

What a prospect is this. There sin is for ever put away. There the whole Church is eternally united without fault or division. There the whole creation shares in the liberty of the glory of the children of God. There the eye sees the King in His beauty; and we shall be like Him, for we shall see Him as He is.

Blessed thought: it shall not always be as it is now. The blessings of the Supper are mere droppings. Jesus Himself comes once for all. Then shall I sit down with Him. Yes, He comes: and I shall see Him and know Him, and He shall see me and know me. And when I fall at His feet He will call me by my name and let me rest on His breast, and take me to be one with Him inseparably and forever.

A Prayer of Thanksgiving to the Holy Trinity

(For the Communion Sabbath Evening)

Triune, God, once again on this blessed feast day I come to pour out my full heart before Thee. I will lift up my soul to Thee in prayer and supplication, and will enjoy anew what Thou hast bestowed upon me, while I praise Thee for it.

Receive my thanks, God and Father of the Lord Jesus, for the wonderful love Thou hast showed to me. That Thou hast prepared for me in Thine heart a place next Thine only-begotten Son, that Thou hast seen meet to honor me with the name and the rights of a child, that Thou hast been pleased to seal to me this privilege all this day by imparting to me the children's; bread: for this my soul desires to praise Thee. O my Father, I will place myself anew before Thee as Thy child, to delight myself in Thee, to dedicate myself to Thee as a living sacrifice:

O my Father, to live wholly for Thee, to honor Thee the whole day with a heart full of joy in Thyself, to keep myself ever burning on the altar as a thank offering by fire: how my heart longs after this. Father, receive the praise, the thanks, the love of the child whom Thou hast this day blessed, and grant me grace to walk from day to day with this song in my heart: "Thanks be to God for His unspeakable gift."

And what shall I say unto Thee, O my Jesus, Son of the Father, for what I have this day again received from Thee. O how I praise Thee for the love wherewith Thou hast loved me. Precious Saviour, Thou hast given Thyself unto me to be mine forever. The bond that unites Thee to me is not broken in eternity; for the bond is Thy love, which is stronger than death. Yea, the bond which Thy love has formed is Thine own Divine life. The life that is in Thee, Thou hast given to be in me: Thou hast made me one with Thyself: I am Thy flesh and bone. Son of God, my soul cannot conceive it: I can only bow in abasement, and surrender myself anew to Thee. O my Lord, Thou desirest to have me wholly: here am I to be wholly taken possession of by Thee, and to be filled with the Spirit whom Thou hast given.

And how shall I praise Thee, O Spirit of the Father and the Son, for what Thou art to me again this day. By Thee I possess and enjoy the Father and the Son. By Thee I taste the powers of the heavenly life. Every blessing which I receive from the Father and the Son I have through Thee. Thou workest in me by Thy Divine power all that I need in the spiritual life. What I have this day received and enjoyed, that Thou hast wrought in me; that Thou wilt preserve and strengthen, till I become fully partaker of the love of the Father and the grace of the Son. O Holy Spirit of God, my soul praises Thee. How long-suffering and patient hast Thou been in spite of all my sluggishness and folly. With the Father and the Son I honor Thee, I love Thee, I delight in Thee and in Thy fellowship.

Triune God of the Covenant, receive this renewed dedication of myself to Thee. Thou art all my salvation, my everlasting portion. O confirm in the most effectual way the sealing of Thy grace bestowed upon me this day, and let me now as Thy sworn ally go hence in the might of the Lord and making mention of Thy righteousness, yea, Thine alone. Amen.

My Prayer for Today:

My Prayer for Today:

PART III
The Week after the Supper

The Lord's Table

Too soon we rise: the symbols disappear.
The feast, though not the love, is past and gone;
The bread and wine remove, but thou art here,
Nearer than ever, still my Shield and Sun.

I have no help but thine: nor do I need
Another arm save Thine to lean upon;
It is enough, my Lord, enough indeed;
My strength is in Thy might, Thy might alone.

Mine is the sin, but Thine the righteousness;
Mine is the guilt, but thine the cleansing blood;
Here is my robe, my refuge and my peace—
Thy blood, Thy righteousness, O Lord my God.

Feast after feast thus comes and passes by,
Yet, passing, points to the glad feast above,
Giving sweet foretaste of the festal joy,
The Lamb's great bridal feast of bliss and love.
—Horatius Bonar.

Monday Morning

Monday Morning
The Power of the Food

"My flesh is meat indeed and My blood is drink indeed. He that eateth My flesh and drinketh My blood abideth in Me and I in Him."—John 6:55.

Life must be fed with life. In corn the life of nature is hid, and we enjoy the power of that life in bread. As with the body, so is it with the spirit. The body is fed by the visible, the changeable life: the spirit must be fed with the invisible, unchangeable life of Heaven.

It was to bring to us this heavenly life that the Son of God descended to earth. It was to make this life accessible to us that He died like the seed corn in the earth, that His body was broken like the bread grain. It is to communicate this life to us and to make it our own, that He gives Himself to us in the Supper.

By His death Jesus took away the cause of our everlasting hunger and sorrow, namely, sin. The spirit of man, his undying part, can live only by God, "who only hath immortality." Sin separated man from God, and an eternal hunger and an eternal thirst of death were now his portion. He lost God, and nothing in the world can satisfy his infinite cravings. Then comes Jesus. He takes sin away and brings it to nought in His body, and gives us that body to eat and to do away with sin in us. Since in Him dwells the fullness of the Godhead bodily, whenever I receive and enjoy Him, not only have I the forgiveness of sins, but the life of God, the life of heaven is implanted within me.

Wonderful grace: may I understand it aright. The man who uses the Lord's Supper aright is one that is distinguished from other men by the fact that he has partaken of the Bread of Life. He has really received Jesus Christ into his innermost being, and with Him the powers of the eternal life, as this is the life of Heaven. It is to bring His own eternal life near to us, that God has given His Son as the food of the soul.

Glorious food: wonderful heavenly bread: what a heavenly life it imparts to us. Love to God, blessed rest, real holiness, inward power, all that characterizes the life that is enjoyed in Heaven,—all that shall be in me the fruit of this Bread of Life.

Let me remember and believe the wonderful virtue of the food with which I am fed. Let me have strong expectations that this food shall work out its divine energy in me. Let me walk joyfully and full of courage, knowing that I can do all things through Christ that strengtheneth me. For He gives me strength. He dwells in me. He is my food.

Prayer

O how wonderful is Thy grace, my precious Lord, that Thou Thyself hast become my food, which abides in me, gives me strength, and upholds and increases the life that is in me.

Lord, I have but one boon to crave of Thee this morning. It is this: that Thou wouldst increase my faith, that I may know aright what Thou art prepared to be to me. I feel that this is especially to be blamed as my weakness that I do not understand what Thou art willing to be and to do for me.

Precious Lord, make me to know this. Strengthen my faith to say continually: Jesus abides in me, Jesus is my food: fed with such nourishment, my life shall be powerful for the glorifying of God. Strengthen my faith to appropriate Thee continually for all my needs. Thou art the Provision in every necessity, the satisfaction of every desire. Strengthen my faith, Lord, to think no more of my weakness but of Thine own power: for Thou, O my Lord, Thou art always my food, my power of life. And strengthen my faith especially to receive this my heavenly food daily as its nourishment, to open my mouth wide every day, in order that it may be filled with Thee, with Thyself.

Lord Jesus, my food, which abides in me, Thou wilt surely do this for me. Amen.

My Prayer for Today:

My Prayer for Today:

Tuesday Morning

Tuesday Morning
Sanctification

"Sin no more."—John 5:14, 8:11.

Thus Jesus spake to the sick man whom He had healed at the pool of Bethesda. Thus He spake also to the woman whom He liberated from the hand of her persecutors. Thus He speaks to every soul to which He has shown mercy, whose sickness He has healed, and whose life He has redeemed from destruction. Thus He speaks to everyone who goes forth from the blessed feast of the Supper: "Go hence: sin no more."

It was in order to save from sin that God sent His Son, that Jesus gave His life and His blood, that the Spirit came down from Heaven. The Redeemer cannot suffer a, ransomed soul to go from the table of the covenant, without hearing anew this glorious word: "Henceforth—let there be no more sin." In the presence of the Cross and what thy sin cost Him, in view of His love and all the blessings which He has bestowed upon you, this Word comes with divine power: "Go hence: sin no more."

"But, Lord, must I not always sin? In me dwelleth no good thing. I thought that the Christian continues to sin to the end."

"And have I not redeemed thee from the power of sin? Does not My Spirit dwell in you? Am not I Myself your sanctification?"

"But, Lord, can anyone, then, in this life be entirely holy?"

"The sinful nature you shall continue to have, but its workings can be overcome. You may become more holy every day. I am prepared to do for you above all that you dare ask or think."

Tuesday Morning - Sanctification

"O my beloved Lord, I would so very fain be holy. *Thou knowest* how sin grieves me, how I pant after holiness. O, pray, teach me how I can be holy."

"Soul, I am thy sanctification. Abide in Me and thou shalt be holy. Entrust thyself to Me: I shall keep you holy. Believe in Me, that I shall fulfill My word. Let My word, My will, My mind, keep thy thoughts, thy heart occupied. Let Me dwell in thine heart—thy heart be full of Me: that will keep sin outside."

"O Lord, may it only be so in my case."

"Soul, fall down before Me, bring thyself to Me in sacrifice. Be not faithless, but believing. Look not upon thy weakness, or upon all that which is dead. Give Me the honor of being strong in faith, and confident that what I have promised, I am mighty and faithful to do, and it shall be to thee according to thy faith."

"Lord, I come. I fall down before Thee to dedicate myself now as a sacrifice to Thee."

Prayer

(of a soul that surrenders itself to the Lord to be purified from every sin)

Blessed Lord, Thou art my sanctification. From Thee I have not only the command, but in Thee the power to go hence and to sin no more. Lord, now I give myself anew to Thee, and declare myself ready to be purified from every sin.

Of every known sin, of which I am already convinced, I do this very moment make renunciation. However deeply it may be rooted, however little I feel power to overcome it, in Thy name, my blessed Redeemer, I Hereby renounce it. I surrender myself to Thee to combat and overcome it in Thy strength. Lord, here am I, in order that Thou mayest cleanse me from all unrighteousness. Lord, this is my prayer: whatever it may cost me, through whatever pain or humiliation it may be achieved, take my sin from me. Lord, spare no single sin: make me holy.

And no less for the sin in me that is still unknown to myself,—sin which Thy people or the world or Thou Thyself mayest see in me, but which my own self-love has not yet been willing to acknowledge, I place myself in

Thy hands. Lord, make it known to me: use friend or foe to discover it, but, pray, let not my sin continue longer hid from me. I would fain know it, in order that I may bring it to Thee, and that Thou mayest cleanse me from it.

And strengthen my faith, precious Saviour, that I may very joyfully reckon on Thee to show Thyself to me as my sanctification. Thou art my Surety, who has not only atoned for the old guilt, but art also in a position to secure that every day and every moment the requirements of God's law may be fulfilled by me. Lord, cause me to believe this, and by a life of unceasing trust to experience how constantly Thou wilt keep and cleanse the soul. Then shall I go away from every observance of the Supper, to show anew that thou art my daily bread, and my daily strength: that Thy life is the life of my life and that Thou hearest my prayer:

"Jesus, come and live in me.

That I may ever, holy be."

Lord, here am I now, surrendered to Thee, to be kept and sanctified in Thee. On Thy word, I confidently cast myself. Amen.

My Prayer for Today:

Wednesday Morning

Wednesday Morning
Obedience

"Jesus said: My meat is to do the will of Him that sent Me, and to finish His work."—John 4:34.

"I have meat to eat that ye know not of." Jesus had a hidden manna that He received from the Father, and that was the secret of His wonderful power. The nutriment of His life He received from God in Heaven. No one could have discovered what it was; but when He tells it to us, it appears so simple that many a one gets puzzled over it. "My meat is to do the will of Him that sent Me, and to finish His work."

Food is the meeting of need, satisfaction. The hunger of Jesus, the yearning of Jesus, extended only to one thing: to please God. Without that He could not rest; in that one thing, He had all He required. And when He found the will of God, He did it, and thereby at once fed His soul with its appropriate food, and was satisfied.

Food involves appropriation, the exercise of fellowship. The weak soul, who truly surrenders himself to do the will of God, becomes thereby wonderfully strengthened. Obedience to God, instead of exhausting the energies, only renews them. The doing of God's will was the food that Jesus had.

Food involves quickening and joy. Eating is not only necessary as medicine for strength, but is also in itself something that is acceptable, and imparts pleasure. To observe a feast in the spirit is itself equivalent to food. Obedience to the will of God was Jesus' highest joy.

As One who did the will of God, Jesus became our Saviour (Heb. 10:9, 10). He therefore that trusts in Him, receives Him as the fulfiller of the will of God, and with Him receives also the will of God as his life.

Now, then, Jesus has become my meat; and He Himself dwells in me as the power of my life. And now I know the means by which this life must be fed and strengthened within me. The doing of God's will is my meat. The doing of God's will was for Jesus the bread of Heaven; and since I have now received Jesus Himself as my heavenly bread, He teaches me to eat what He Himself ate: He teaches me to do the will of God. That is the meat of my soul. I received the same Spirit that was in Him, and it became truth for me, as for Him. My meat, the highest satisfaction of my soul, fellowship with God, renewal of my energies, an unbroken feast of joy, is "to do the will of Him that sent me, and to finish His work." Thus the feast of the Supper is prolonged in the continued life of obedience to the will of God.

Prayer

Eternal God, I thank Thee that in Thy Son Thou hast enabled us here on earth to contemplate the glorious life of heaven. I thank Thee for the sight of Him who, in the execution of Thy will found His meat, His life. Lord God, in the Supper Thou hast given me this Son in order that His life may become my life, and His Spirit my spirit. Lord, make me so thoroughly one with this Jesus, that I also, like Him, shall find my meat in the will of the Father.

Lord Jesus, it is a continued feast that Thou hast prepared for me. Every day I also may do the will of my Father. May this obedience be to me the continuation of the banquet of the Supper. Make my soul crave with an insatiable hunger to know the will of God in everything. Do Thou Thyself with Thy Divine power fulfill in me all obedience, and let my inner life thereby become all the stronger and more joyful.

Lord, I desire to confess before Thee how little I still have of true spiritual insight into the will of God. Lord, give me of Thy Spirit, in order that I may be transformed by the renewing of my mind, and so prove what is that good and perfect and acceptable will of God. Bring me to that blessed frame of mind in which, like Thee, my Lord, I shall refuse to do anything, unless I know that it is the will of the Father. Strengthen my faith, that by the Spirit Thou mayest make me to understand this will more fully, and in order that I may stand perfect and complete in all the will of God.

O, my Saviour, how shall my soul then be satisfied and

praise Thee when all that I do is only obedience to the prayer: "Our Father, Thy will be done, as in Heaven so on earth."

Lord, give me always this food. Amen.

My Prayer for Today:

My Prayer for Today:

Thursday Morning

Thursday Morning
Work

"If any will not work, neither let him eat."—2 Thessalonians 3:10.

That is true of the poor sluggard: he has nothing to eat. It is also true of the hireling: he cannot expect that his master will give him food to eat if he does not do his work. It is also true of the rich sluggard: although he has abundance, if he does not work he lacks the hunger that makes food acceptable.

And it is no less true, on the other hand, of spiritual food. The Kingdom of God is not meat and drink: there least of all may the bread of idleness be eaten. Israel had to eat the Passover, with loin girt, sandals on the feet, and staff in hand, ready to undertake the journey to Canaan in the strength of the food enjoyed.

Now, may not this fact discover to us the reason why, for many, the blessing imparted at the Supper is not greater than it is? They desire to partake of it in order to have an enjoyable festal hour, to be satisfied with blessed pleasures and glorious experiences. But they do not reflect that the Lord has prepared food for His children that they may be strengthened to go and work in His vineyard. They do not work for their Lord: they do not know what they ought to do: they do not consider the matter: and thus they have often to complain of darkness and loss of blessing at the Lord's Supper.

"If any will not work, neither let him eat": "If any will work, let him eat."

Alike in nature and in grace there is one law. He that desires to eat for the sake only of getting the food and for the satisfaction of his appetite, shall speedily lose the enjoyment of the food. He that eats to become strong and to work, shall find the food always accompanied with relish and imparting strength.

Thursday Morning - Work

Christian, once again you have eaten: now is the time for work. Work the work of your Lord: live and work for the interests of His kingdom, and He will see to it that you have your food, and that the food will prove to you a source of relish and blessing. As it is in the service of an earthly parent, so is it in that of the Heavenly Father: the best preparation for the Lord's Supper is to have done faithfully the will of the Father, and to have finished His work. It was when Abraham returned from the campaign for the deliverance of Lot that Melchisedek, the priest of the Most High God, set before him bread and wine. "To him that overcometh," says Jesus—to him that works and strives and overcomes—"will I give to eat of the hidden manna."

Prayer

Holy Lord my Redeemer and my Friend, it is my desire to work for Thee. I know that Thou hast given Thyself for us for this end, that Thou mightest have us for Thyself a peculiar people, zealous of good works. I know that there is no blessedness save in doing the will of the Father and finishing the work: He has given me. Lord, I come to Thee, in the joy and courage and power that the food which Thou Thyself hast prepared as the nutriment of my soul imparts, to ask of Thee my work.

I believe, Lord, that there is work for me, and that Thou wilt point out that work to me. Often have I desired to work for Thee according to my own feelings, and I have failed to win success. Lord Jesus, do Thou point out to me the work that I must do. Thou art my food and my strength. Thou art also my light and my leader. Let Thy Spirit so dwell in me that I shall be able to discern His voice, and, stimulated by Him, may carry out my work for souls.

Lord, I have eaten the bread of Heaven: I will live to do the work of Heaven. Heavenly food brings heavenly strength, and heavenly strength brings heavenly work. Lord, make me to be Thy fellow-laborer, and teach me, like Thyself, to give my life to the work of the Kingdom of Heaven. Let my greatest joy be like that which prevails in heaven over the sinner that repenteth.

Thursday Morning - Work

That work will cause me to feel the need of Thy divine power. That work will prepare me also to enjoy Thy food aright. That work will make every observance of the Supper more glorious for me, as a still deeper exercise of communion with Thee. So be it, O my Lord. Amen.

My Prayer for Today:

Friday Monday

Friday Morning
Fellowship with Jesus

*"And lo, I am with you alway (*all the days*), even unto the end of the world."*—Matthew 28:20.

"For you": that was one of the words of Jesus at the table.

"With you": this is no less His promise, when you go away from the table. As real and complete and certain as His suretyship was, when He bore sin and gave His life for you, so real and certain is the fellowship which He holds out to you when He says, "I am *with you* all the days." If the "*for you*" was in every respect undivided and all sufficient, He means the "with you" to be in every respect just as undivided and inseparable.

And the one is, like the other, *a word of faith*: a word that unfolds itself only to faith. "*For you*" was in the first instance a truth that you found it impossible to receive. But the Spirit of God brought you up to the point of reception, and you were enabled to say, "Yes: Jesus for me—in my place: it is all finished for me." And this is now the sure and deep confidence of your soul. Even thus shall it be with this other word, "*with you.*" Too often it appears as if it were not true, as if it could not possibly be true. At other times you could not live long if you felt yourself to be so sinful and miserable as you are. And yet it is true that *Jesus is with you.* Only you do not know it, you do not enjoy it, because you *do not believe it.* But as soon as you learn to rely, not upon your own feeling or on your own experience, but on what He has promised, and to direct your expectations according to faith in that which He hath said, namely, that He will be with you, it will become your blessedness. The "with you" is just as certain and complete as the "for you."

"*I am with you.*" Jesus Himself abides with His own: the certainty of His presence and love, which will not abandon us. He, the Living, the Loving, the Almighty One: He Himself is with us, and in a position to make Himself known to us.

"With you all the days:" not only on the day of the Supper; not only on the festal days of life; but all the days, without one single exception. And thus, also, all the day. Whether I think of it or not, there He is the whole day—near me, with me. Not on my own faithfulness, but in that faithfulness of Thine which awakens my confidence and bestows on me Thine own nearness, I have the assurance of an unbroken fellowship with Thee, my beloved Lord.

Prayer

Blessed Saviour, receive my thanks also for this word, "with you." And teach me, Lord, to make it my own in faith. For this end I will during these moments set myself in silence before Thee, and will wait upon Thee. Lord, speak Thyself to me these words "I am with you all the days."

Lord, what a source of joy and strength shall it prove to me when I know that as Thou art unchangeable, so also is Thy presence with me unchangeable. As little as Thou wilt for a single moment leave the right hand of the Father in Heaven, wilt Thou leave Thy brother upon the earth: Thou abidest at my right hand. Thou hast said it, and therefore I know that it is true: "I will never leave you nor forsake you I am with you all the days." Precious Saviour, let Thy voice penetrate into the deepest recesses of my heart, and let my life this day, the whole day, and every day, be in Thy presence the presence of Him who says, "I am with you."

Alas, Lord, what have I not lost by not believing that word! And how have I grieved and dishonored Thee. Thou wast with me: Thy voice of love said without ceasing, "I am with you"; and yet through my proneness to unbelief, I heard it not. Often did I pray and beseech Thee that I might have Thee, and yet at the same time I practically despised Thee by not believing Thy Word. O my Saviour, let it no longer be so. Strengthen my faith, and as Thou has taught me to rely upon the Word of complete atonement, "For you," let the word of complete fellowship, "with you all the days," become my joy and my strength. Yea, cause me to understand that as the "for you" makes a complete provision for all the sins of the past, so the "with you" makes a provision equally complete for all the cares and sins of the future.

Yes, Lord, in Thy strength it shall be so. I will trust and not be afraid. Whatever or of whatever kind the days may be that await me, Thy word, "*with you all the days*," shall be sufficient for me. In Thy nearness, in fellowship with Thee, or rather in Thy fellowship with me, my life shall become a foretaste of the consummation when I shall say: "And lo, O Lord, I am with Thee for all eternity!" Amen.

My Prayer for Today:

My Prayer for Today:

Saturday Morning

Saturday Morning
The End

"The Lord will perfect that which concerneth me." "Being confident of this very thing, that He which began a good work in you will perfect it until the day of Jesus Christ." Psalm 138:8; Philippians 1:6.

How many times has the believer gone from the Lord's Table with the sorrowful thought, Shall I indeed continue standing? Shall my resolutions and promises not be frustrated? Who tells me that I shall persevere unto the end? *"I shall now perish one day by the hand of Saul"* (1 Samuel 27:1).

It was just in such a crisis that David said, *"I will cry unto God Most High, unto God that performeth all things for me"* (Ps. 57:2). It is in God alone that the Christian has the assurance of his perseverance. To see from the beginning to the end, yea, to be Himself alike "the Beginning and the End," is one of the glorious attributes of the God who dwells in eternity. And it is one of the characteristics of His work, that, while man often begins without ending, with Him the end is as certain as the beginning. "What He has begun He will complete."

O my soul, if thou wouldst enjoy the comfort of this promise, be much occupied with this fact: "He has begun." The Christian speaks too often of his conversion and his faith and his self-surrender. Contemplating all this from the side of man, he keeps himself too little occupied with the thought: "HE has begun." My soul, understand what this means: He has sought me and found me and made me His own, and what He has thus done to me points back to that which He did for me: He gave His own Son, and by His blood He bought for Himself as His own possession. And that again points back to eternity. He chose me and loved me before the foundation of the world. My soul, ponder what this means: "He has begun."

Then shalt thou be able joyfully to exclaim, "He will perfect:" "the Lord will perfect that which concerneth me." Then shalt thy life become a life of humility and thanksgiving and confidence and joy and love. Thou seest that there is nothing in thyself, and thou learnest to expect all from God, and thank Him for all: thou learnest to rely upon Him in everything. And the end will be to you as certain as the beginning, because the end as well as the beginning has its root and stability in God. The self-same faith that, looking back, acknowledges the beginning as God's, also looks forward, and in the eternal and unchangeable God finds the end secured. "What He has begun He will perfect."

Prayer

Lord God, Thou art without beginning and without end. For Thou art Thyself alike the beginning and the end. Thou art the Eternal, with whom there is no yesterday and no to-morrow. Thou art Thyself yesterday, today, and forever. With Thee there is no changeableness nor shadow of turning. Lord, in Thee alone Thy believing people find their comfort and their security. Nothing that we have done or still desire to do, nothing that we are or shall be, can give us rest. But, thanks be to Thy name, Thou Thyself, the Eternal, with Thine unchangeableness, Thou art our rest and our strength, In Thee alone and in Thy faithfulness does our life become freed from all fear.

Father, give me to understand this. Make me to know Thee as the God who has begun a good work in me. Let Thy Spirit seal it to me that Thou receivest me as the possession which Thou hast bought for Thyself, which is precious to Thee, and which no one shall pluck out of Thy hands. And then teach me, in the midst of all the sense of my own weakness and the power of sin which I have, always to trust and always to exclaim: "He that began a good work in me will perfect it."

Father, once again I thank Thee for the Supper that has been observed. Blessed Perfecter, perfect in me also Thy work of grace. Teach me to go forward on my way, full of joy, full of confidence and courage, full of thanksgiving and love. My God, become Thou everything to me: the God who has done everything, the God who will do everything, the God to whom all is due. and give me thereafter to await the glorious end, when I too shall be in perfection what I was at the beginning, and every day hope more and more to be, a monument of the grace of God on which he that runneth may read: "From Him and by Him and to Him are all things: to Him be glory for ever and ever." Amen.

My Prayer for Today:

APPENDIX

Throughout the preceding pages the author makes such pointed reference to the statements of the Directory of Public Worslnp in the Dutch Reformed Church that bear on preparation for the Lord's Supper, and also to the relevant questions of the Heidelberg Catechism, that it has been thought of advantage to the reader to have these passages before him.

I. Self-Examanation

True proving of ourselves consists of three parts:—

1. In the first place, let everyone in his own heart reflect on his sin and condemnation, in order that he may loathe himself and humble himself before God: seeing that the wrath of God against sin is so great that, rather than suffer it to remain unpunished, He punished it in His dear Son Jesus Christ, in the bitter and ignominous death of the Cross.

2. In the second place, let everyone examine his heart as to whether he also believes this sure promise of God, that only on the ground of the suffering and death of Jesus Christ all his sins are forgiven him, and the perfect righteousness of Christ is bestowed upon him and imputed to him as his own: yea, as completely as if he himself in his own person had atoned for all his sins and performed all righteousness.

3. In the third place, let everyone examine his conscience as to whether he is prepared, henceforth and with his whole life, to manifest true thankfulness toward God the Lord, and to walk uprightly in God's sight.

"All who are so disposed, God will assuredly receive into His favor, and regard as worthy communicants at the table of His Son Jesus Christ. On the other hand, those that have no such testimony in their hearts, eat and drink judgment to themselves."

II. Christ in the Supper

Question 76: What is meant by eating the crucified body and drinking the shed blood of Christ?

Answer: It is not only to receive with a believing heart the whole suffering and dying of Christ, and thereby to obtain the forgiveness of sins and life eternal, but moreover, also, to be so united more and more to His sacred body by the Holy Ghost, who dwells both in Christ and in us, that although He is in Heaven and we are upon the earth, we are nevertheless flesh of His flesh and bone of His bones, and live and are governed forever by One Spirit, as the members of one body are by one soul.

Question 79: Why, then, doth Christ call the bread His body and the cup His blood, or the New Testament in His blood; and St. Paul, the communion of the body and blood of Christ?

Answer: Christ speaks thus not without great cause, namely, not only that He may thereby teach us that like as bread and wine sustain this temporal life, so also His crucified body and shed blood are the true meat and drink of our souls unto eternal life; but, much more that by this visible sign and pledge He may assure us that we are as really partakers of His true body and blood, through the working of the Holy Spirit, as with the bodily mouth we receive these holy tokens in remembrance of Him; and that all His suffering and obedience are as surely our own as if we ourselves in our own person had suffered all and done enough.

More Classic books available from Destiny Image Publishers

A Short and Easy Method of Prayer
by Madame Guyon

Paradise Lost *by John Milton*

The Possibilities of Prayer *by EM Bounds*

Purpose in Prayer *by Edward Bounds*

The Essentials of Prayer *by Edward Bounds*

The Lords Table *by Andrew Murray*

All of Grace *by Charles Haddon Spurgeon*

Dark Night of the Soul *by St. John of the Cross*

Paradise Regained *by John Milton*

Power Through Prayer *by EM Bounds*

Prayer and Praying Man *by EM Bounds*

The Deeper Christian Life *by Andrew Murray*

The New Life *by Andrew Murray*

The Autobiography *of Madame Guyon*

Grace Abounding to the Chief of Sinners
by John Bunyan

The Marriage of Heaven and Hell *by William Blake*

The Necessity of Prayer *by EM Bounds*

The Practice of the Presence of God
by Brother Lawrence

The Reality of Prayer *by EM Bounds*

The Weapon of Prayer *by EM Bounds*